IDENTITY CRISIS

*The Debilitating Disease
of the Church*

BISHOP JOHN K. VINCENT

Identity Crisis: *The Debilitating Disease of the Church*

Copyright © 2025 Bishop John K. Vincent

ISBN (Paperback): 978-1-964494-83-8
ISBN (Ebook): 978-1-964494-84-5

Printed in the United States of America.

PROMINENT
BOOKS

5830 E 2nd St, Ste 7000 #9983
Casper, WY 82609
USA

"And call no man your father upon the earth: for one is your Father, which is in heaven."

—Matthew 23:9

CONTENTS

INTRODUCTION

Recent studies have revealed that fewer people are attending public worship gatherings, and instead are searching for personal identity in their spiritual journey. Many have disassociated themselves from organized religion because of unfulfilled needs or disappointment! The reality is that many people began exiting the physical church building before the global exodus during Covid-19, and many are continuing to leave. Albeit very alarming, much of this trend is attributed to what I consider to be a major shift in Christendom, including a downward spiral and exposing of corrupt leaders who hold positions of influence within the church. Consequently, this widespread phenomenon has provoked many to examine the relevance of the 21st Century church, and to question its future identity. Has the church age as we've known it come to an end?

Many of the scandals and improprieties that have been exposed in religion, stem from a rise of ungodly men and women, who engage in activities that misrepresent the sanctity and sacredness of the Kingdom of God. It's important to observe that the church has embraced a new liturgical paradigm, while yet navigating through the past residue of entrenched indoctrination and tradition. If you really want to know the truth, a major shifting and sifting is occurring, and new leaders are emerging. God is raising leaders that truly understand their assignment!

The influence that a leader has over people should never be more important than the impact they make in the people lives that they lead. The ultimate goal is to live an effective life in word and deed, bringing glory and honor to God. Pastors are called by God to shepherd and to lead those entrusted under their watch care, protecting the flock from erroneous teachings, and guiding them in the paths of righteousness. It is very important for every leader to understand the power of their voice and the clarity of their assignment, and that spiritual authority does not replace or dismiss divine identity.

Many of you may be familiar with the term *"Spiritual Father", it is an identity in religion* which in my opinion is a misused expression of piety, and a misrepresentation of spiritual identity. This school of thought has undeniably perpetuated a systemic cycle of spiritual, physical, sexual, emotional, and even financial abuse within the church, causing many people to question the legitimacy of spiritual authority, and most importantly the legitimacy of one's true spiritual identity in Christ Jesus.

It is incumbent of me as a Bishop, but most importantly servant-leader to humbly share my convictions regarding this dangerous issue, and to provide some biblical and practical insight concerning an identity crisis that has negatively affected the image of the church.

The purpose of this book is not to incite a theological or religious argument amongst *leadership, for God is not the author of confusion but of peace*; Neither is it the purpose to publically indict the church, but rather to help shift the mentality of some, and to stimulate the minds of others concerning a very pressing and prominent issue in both the Catholic and Protestant reformations. It is my humble desire to provide a biblical measure for 21st century Christian leadership, spiritual and mutual accountability, and an evaluation of how leaders use their sphere of influence in religion.

"A person who won't read has no advantage over one who can't read."

—Mark Twain

CHAPTER ONE
"Manipulation Disguised in Religion"

The freedom to practice organized religion in America is both a constitutional right and an individual privilege, however that freedom should never be used to abuse, manipulate or prey upon the vulnerable!—It's sad to say that some have used religion as a disguise for abusing and misusing others for selfish gain!

Did you know that the unauthorized use of someone's personal information, such as their name is considered *identity theft, and is usually punishable by law, including fines and or imprisonment?* Are you aware that a published false statement that is damaging to a person's reputation is more than just a misrepresentation of the truth, but is also considered to be *libel*, and is subject to impending legal consequences? Furthermore, the willful act of manipulation and control from any person, particularly those in a position of authority, is considered an abuse of power and bullying; both of which are commonly associated with an individual's own insecurity and inner struggle for power and control. These types of behaviors are unacceptable and will be judged by God!

To be very clear, not everyone in the faith community are imposters looking for opportunity to harm others, but everyone does have their own respective issues to battle. Whether it's an issue of lust, or an issue of greed, we all have flaws! Nobody is exempt from being tempted by their own lustful desires, wicked imaginations, and demonic influences of Satan. *James 1:14 says, "But every man is tempted, when he is drawn away of his own lust, and enticed."*

However, there are some people who have disguised their identity, and are using that disguise to entice and entrap others. They may appear to have good intentions, but in reality they have hidden motives, and their main objective is to get what they want, even at the expense of harming others. People who practice these egregious behaviors oftentimes leave their victims in permanent ruin. Unfortunately, this has been the narrative within the world, the church world I might add, and as a result, many today are in search of recovering their true identity in God. *1 John 4:1 says, "Beloved, believe not every spirit, but try the spirits whether they are of God: because many of false prophets are gone out into the world."*

People who pretend to be someone in order to deceive and control others for fraudulent gain, are called imposters. These type of people are very dangerous individuals, and they enjoy manipulating others at any cost. They typically are narcissist who think very highly of themselves, and see other people as being inferior to them. Unfortunately, many of these characteristics are seen rampant throughout religious entities, and has affected countless of lives in ways we've never imagined. There are so many tragic stories that have been exposed, and yet so many more that have not ever been reported.

It takes a lot of courage and wisdom from the Holy Spirit to address some of the indoctrinated traditions and ideologies of religion that have been passed down from generations. Religious leaders of both the Catholic and Protestant reformations hold a very sacred place of influence and identity in the lives of their respective parish. However, neither of those positions should ever be used to manipulate or misrepresent those who are submitted under their leadership authority. The assumed notion that some individuals are inherently equal to the divine nature of our eternal God is not only disturbing, but very damaging to the image of Christ. This perception has woefully contributed to a very dangerous and disabling culture within the church body worldwide.

Our spiritual son-ship is in God through Christ Jesus. *Having been adopted into the family of God our heavenly (spiritual) Father, we are his heirs (children), and joint heirs with Jesus Christ, (our elder brother)*. It is vitally important that people understand the difference between a *spiritual covering* and *"Spiritual Father."* One must never confuse earthly assignment with divine authority, whether intentionally or unintentionally. When people identify their leader as *spiritual father*, it opens up a wide door of vulnerability that has proven over history to be very detrimental in the lives of many.

The church as an institution has certainly evolved since its' early inception. We have witnessed a decline on most Sunday morning's *(Saturday morning's, if you are Seventh Day Adventist)*, in church attendance and member engagement. This is not solely due to the pandemic, although it has obviously contributed. Some millennials between the ages of 18–35 have practically lost interest in gathering weekly for worship to hear a divine-inspired message. Some perhaps are staying home and watching their favorite T.V. preacher, while others are relying on their own knowledge.

A research conducted by the *Hartford Institute of Religion* says, "40 percent of Americans say they go to church weekly, however less than 20 percent are actually in church." In fact, another study by the *Pew Research Center* shows that 70.6 percent of adults identify themselves as Christians, and 46.5 percent say they attend a variety of churches that are considered protestant. These staggering statistics continue to change!

As a result, many leaders of congregations have been challenged to make adjustments in how services are facilitated through the advanced technology of social media, such as Facebook, Periscope, Twitter, and Instagram to name a few. Some have gone to great extremes to remain connected and relevant to their congregants, using various means to keep the engagement of their following. Yes, I believe it's fair to say that we indeed have an Identity Crisis within the church culture!

Every person, whether they acknowledge it or not desires to know their true identity. Somewhere deep within the recesses of our minds, we all want to know who we are, where we came from, why we are here, and most importantly where we are going. It's been said, *a person who does not know where they came from, most likely don't know where they are going.* People have suffered with anxiety, depression, drug addictions, anger issues, control issues, self-esteem issues, trust issues, sexual issues, gender issues, and the list goes on; all in quest of finding their identity.

The influence of social norms, political parties, and the power of public opinion has undoubtedly contributed to the identity crisis of our global world, and the church world is not excluded. Humanity as a whole is easily influenced by the popularity of others, and oftentimes become vulnerable to those who sometimes may have hidden agendas. Throughout history we have seen government corruption, manipulation by the mainstream media, and a downward spiraling of morality. In addition, we have observed the breakdown of the family unit which has spilled over into our communities. The world has normalized behaviors that was once considered abnormal! Yes indeed, we have an identity crisis.

For years we have witnessed the unfortunate reality of the absentee fathers in the home, and the adverse effect it has had on our children and community. Mothers have been forced to take on a role that they were never meant to embrace, as well as an identity that they could never live up to, no matter how hard they tried. Let's take a look at some other statistics:

According to the *U.S. census bureau*, 24 million children, that is 1 out of 3, live without their biological father in the home. As a result, a child has a four times greater risk of living in poverty, two time greater risk of infant mortality, seven times likely to become pregnant as a teen, and two time more likely to drop out of school. In fact, Mississippi has the highest number of children living without a father in the home, followed by Louisiana and Alabama.

Can you imagine growing up without a father? I'm talking about the man who not only impregnated your mother with his seed, but also carried the X and Y chromosome that gave all of his children their *"gender identity."* I'm talking about the kind of father who is supposed to be the protector and provider for his family. *Where are these fathers today?* Some are exactly where they are supposed to be, involved in their children's life. Unfortunately, the harsh reality for many children is that their father is *MIA (Missing in action). When fathers are missing, their children tend to look for validation and approval from the wrong people!* This is why so many of our youth are troubled and involved in all sorts of criminal activity.

It's fair to say that the absentee father has directly contributed to the breakdown of the *traditional* family unit within society. God's original plan for human creation was to have both father and mother raising their children together. According to Genesis 2:24, a man is to leave his father and mother, and to cleave or to be *joined* to his wife. The two of them would become one, and reproduce after their kind. A father is so much more than just a donor of his seed! Fathers are men who embrace the great responsibility of leading, feeding, guiding, and most importantly loving their children. *A "real daddy" teaches his sons how to be men, and his daughter's how to be treated by men.* It's the father's responsibility to set good standards for his family, and for those standards to be passed down to future generations.

Perhaps you know your father, but the relationship with him is so estranged and distant that you wish you never did! Maybe your father was very condescending and abusive to your mother, and she was forced to raise all of the children alone. God forbid that you were molested by your father or even a close family member who took advantage of you, and robbed you of your innocence. *I think you get my point that people all over the world are confronted with various identity crises, and everyone is affected in one way or another!*

There are many different scenarios concerning identity crisis in our society, but we will address a specific issue related to the identity of leadership in the church. The Church has had a major influence in shaping and developing many of the fundamental doctrinal beliefs and practices. It has been the backbone of our respective communities for many years, and has influenced countless of lives throughout our country's history.

However, what I'm about to share will probably challenge some peoples religious beliefs and philosophy. Nevertheless, I believe that every person who reads and understands the context of this subject, and the spirit in which it is presented, will be liberated in their mentality, and able to help others reclaim their true *spiritual identity!*

"Reckless Religion" is the kind of belief that breeds contempt in the eyes of God, and may cause others to disassociate or contemplate their Christianity. It is irresponsible for a generation to perpetuate an ideology or belief system that is counterproductive to the growth and development of the foundational truths of God's holy word. One of the greatest tragedies in life is pretending to be something or someone that you're not, and living a life under false pretense, which is called living a lie! It is unnecessary in the body of Christ to live a disguised identity. God does not want you impersonating him nor any other individual. In the words of Shakespeare's play, Hamlet—*"To thine own self be true, and it must follow, as the night the day, thou canst not then be false to any man."*

"Manipulation is a contagious disease, much more dangerous than the flu because it can endure for a lifetime."

—DorothyMcCoy

CHAPTER TWO
"The Science of Church Psychology"

N ewton's laws of motion in physics says, for every action, there is an equal or opposite reaction. The law of gravity states whatever goes up must eventually come down. God's word however says, whatever is done in the dark shall be brought to the light! The physical and psychological makeup of the church culture for many years has been about the art of persuasion; an ability to influence behavior of an audience, to produce a specific outcome.

Our race, culture, customs, environment, and socio-economic status all play a significant role in shaping our behavior, perception, and beliefs. Psychology addresses the scientific study of the human mind and its respective functions, particularly those affecting the mental and emotional factors. The knowledge of church psychology is beneficial to the awareness of the various schemes perpetrated by masterminds in the pulpit.

One might ask, why discuss the psychology of the church, and how is it related to this *Identity Crisis* within the Church Culture? First, it is what has been displayed to the masses for century. Secondly, it is important to understand the history of the church in order to comprehend the present state of the church. To ease your mind, this book is not for the purpose of promoting racial, cultural, or socio-economic divide within the church of our Lord Jesus Christ, (although on most Sunday's that's exactly what happens), but rather to inform and enlighten how church culture has changed over the years as a result of certain learned behaviors. Furthermore, it is not to criticize the traditional framework of the church, but rather to address an issue that has been predominantly associated within the African American culture.

In the early history of slavery, blacks were segregated from whites, and were not permitted to attend their church services. Unfortunately, many blacks didn't even know how to read or write during this time, so they were very limited in understanding about their religious practices. Some slave master's later taught their slaves how to read which played a very significant part in the way scriptures were interpreted from the Bible. As a result, the slaves blindly trusted the words and teachings expressed by their leader without having complete understanding.

Certain scriptures were used in that day by the master as a means of manipulating and controlling the slaves. For example, *Ephesians 6:5 says, "Servants, (also translated as slaves), be obedient to them that are your masters according to the flesh, with fear and trembling, in singleness of your heart, as unto* Christ." Scriptural text like this have been used to mislead and influence behavior, giving some leadership opportunity to perpetuate the slave master relationship, which is a subservient position.

Times have certainly changed with regards to how people revere leadership. Most people today are much more learned and less trusting than in times past. According to the *African American Registry*, the Black Church, which dates back to November 1, 1758, was the first source of official land ownership for slaves in America. Having been an oppressed people for many decades, they were finally permitted to assemble and have their own worship services. This was a form of emotional relief and release for blacks from the repression and stress of their white slave master's.

Many whites observed closely when blacks came together for their religious gatherings because they believed it was an opportunity for them to escape or revolt, which would be an ultimate threat to white existence. In fact, one slave is said to have recalled that whites would come in to the colored's prayer meeting, and start whipping every one of them because they assumed the prayers were against them. The first recorded Black church in America was called the African Baptist or "Bluestone" church, which was founded on the William Byrd plantation in Mecklenburg, Virginia. This plantation has been designated as a part of the National Historic Landmark in the United States. However, the "First African Baptist Church" of Savannah, Georgia, which began in 1777, is said to be the oldest Black church in North America.

The African Methodist Episcopal Church, which is abbreviated A.M.E. was founded in 1816 by Richard Allen and his colleagues, and is the first independent Protestant denomination to be founded by black people. Its headquarters is in Nashville, Tennessee and they claim to have between 2.5 and 3.5 million members. After the Civil War, Black Baptists desired to practice Christianity separate from racial discrimination and set up separate churches and state Baptist conventions. In 1866, black Baptist of the South and West formed the consolidated American Baptist Convention, which unfortunately later collapsed. However, in 1895 three conventions merged to create the National Baptist Convention, which is now the largest African-American religious organization in the United States.

William J. Seymour was a black influential preacher who traveled to Los Angeles and began a three-year-long Azusa Street Revival in 1906. This movement of integrated and racial equality attracted many people, including a Baptist minister from Arkansas named Charles Harrison Mason. Mason who had a vision from the Lord concerning the church, would later encounter Seymour and experience the baptism of the Holy Ghost with the evidence of speaking in tongues while at the Azusa Street revival, and this became known as the birthing of the Pentecostal movement. The Church of God in Christ, which is the largest Pentecostal denomination in the world, and has over six million members worldwide, was founded in 1907 by Bishop Charles Harrison Mason.

Today, there are many denominations and non-denominations, of which all share their respective values in Christendom. However, since the emergence of various black denominations, we have seen over the past centuries an erroneous ideology, the likes of which may stem from a history of a subservient mentality. Some leaders of the church have adopted the mentality of a monarchy, which is absolute control over the people that they lead. Some will question if this is learned behavior, or just an art of manipulation. One thing that certainly holds true today as it did years ago, there is a profound loyalty to ignorance. People can perceive that something is not right but will continue to stay in it because of their loyalty to a personality or an organization.

The overstepping of spiritual boundaries has contributed to an increase of *church hurt* and dysfunction in the world, leaving many people confused, heart-broken, and powerless. In the Catholic Church you find that priests are recognized as the *"holy father"*, and those who regularly practice Catholicism confess their sins to a priest behind a veil for pardoning and atonement of their sins.

To the contrary, those who are of the protestant faith believes that God is the *Holy Father*, and that anyone can come boldly before the throne of grace to obtain help and mercy in the time of need, according to Hebrews 4:15–16. However, there is a major challenge in the *identity and position of spiritual authority*. When one does not know who they are in Christ, they become whatever and whoever others designate them to be.

The African American Church experience for example has been perceived as one of the most charismatic, energetic, and entertaining gatherings on Sunday mornings. People are often amazed by the creative expressions of praise and worship, such as the high-spirited congregational songs, the demonstrative choir director, the theatrical arts and dancing, and of course the in your face kind of preaching.

This unexplainable energy is both an exhilarating and startling phenomenon that stems from a very rich legacy of ancestral influence. There is a resounding *sound* that comes from the inner depths of the heart and soul of the *African American* culture, and reaches the very core of ones' emotions. It's an occurrence and impression that can't be described in mere words alone. However, the experience has had such great influence on our psyche, which comprises of the human soul, mind, or spirit; and although experience is not always the best teacher in life, it does certainly have a way conditioning the mind.

The mind is the element or consciousness of a person that enables them to be aware of their environment and respective experiences. When an individual is not conscious or aware of their environment, they become susceptible to deception and trickery of others.

"No matter the situation, never allow your emotions to overpower your intelligence"

—Unknown

CHAPTER THREE
"The Origin of Identity Crisis"

E verything and everyone has an origin! The origin is the point or place where something began or originated. We all can reflect on the story of creation in Genesis Chapter One, when God created the heavens and the earth. Everything he created was done in systematic order and according to his divine command. God later made man in his own image and likeness, giving him creative ingenuity and power to create.

Let's pivot for a quick moment and take a look at one specific entity man created, namely denominations. A denomination, within the context of the Protestant faith is a branch of the Christian church that is recognized autonomously by its position as it relates to faith and doctrine. A denomination has its respective qualities and values that give its unique identity, but the most significant question to ask is, are those qualities and values productive or counterproductive? Do they help to unite the Body of Christ or divide it?

Pentecostalism for example, is the denomination of which I grew up, and my core values and beliefs are directly tied to that experience. Many of those core values and beliefs are deep-rooted traditions which continue to evolve this present day. The Pentecostal experience has had a major influence in Christendom, as it celebrates and embraces the power of the Holy Spirit which was released on the Day of Pentecost, in Acts Chapter Two. Having been raised in a predominately black Pentecostal experience has provided a solid spiritual foundation, of which I continue to build upon today. One of the many things I've discovered about my journey of faith is, it is both an individual and collective venture.

I can remember when saints went to church, and they actually wanted to be there! They stayed for hours singing songs, shouting and dancing before the Lord, testifying of the goodness of Jesus, and listening to the unadulterated gospel preached boldly! Preaching back then was not as philosophical and scripted in its presentation, but it was very authentic and certainly anointed. The saints of old took their time in celebrating and worshipping the Lord, and even if they didn't get it right, many of them were sincere! I yet cherish those precious memories today.

I have both heard and witness a lot of things happen in the church, some of which I was directly involved, and others that I only observed from a distance. As I reflect a half of century of life, I can remember years ago as child, whenever the head leader of the church would walk into the sanctuary, everyone would stand in reverence. As a youth, I often wondered why we had to pause and stand to our feet when the *"Chief Apostle"* entered the sanctuary. Someone could be up testifying or singing a song, and right in the middle of their testimony or song, the presiding Bishop would enter the sanctuary, kneel down to pray, and then be seated.

One of the service facilitators would stop the service abruptly and announce for everyone to stand in acknowledgment of the Senior Presiding Bishop. As a young person, it seemed a little strange, but as I matured, I later understood that it was a form of respect and honor for leadership. I do believe it's in order to show respect for leadership! If the President of United States walks into a room, everyone must rise to honor him. If a judge walks to his or her bench, everyone must rise to give respect to them. Why not the Man of God, even greater?

I can remember so clearly my late Father, Bishop John Vincent Jr would leave every year in August to go to the National Convocation, leaving our mother and children behind because he was obligated to be there early. Having served as the National Secretary for some 26 years, and later as a *Prelate Diocese Bishop*, he demonstrated a profound loyalty to the Church! In fact, many of the Saints were loyal to church and to the leadership of the church, giving homage to the spiritual head. According to scripture it is biblical to give honor to whom honor is due.—Romans 13:7 says, *"Render therefore to all their dues: tribute to whom tribute is due; custom to whom custom; fear to whom fear; honor to whom honor."* However, one thing I have observed over the years is that people can cross the boundaries of honor, and it can very quickly turn into idolatry, which is the worship of another person. *Remember, whatever or whoever you worship becomes your God!*

As a leader, I understand the seat of authority of which I operate, and the great responsibility that comes with overseeing God's people. I further understand that I am a representation of God's message to those under my leadership, even as Moses was to the children of Israel. Interestingly, some people have crossed the boundaries of spiritual leadership, placing themselves in an unsanctioned position of authority that exceeds scriptural authority.

I once subscribed to the term "spiritual father" because it was the common expression in the church culture of which I was exposed. It sounded theologically correct, and it was a term of deference that honored the person in your life that spiritually birthed you into the family of God. But I had a revelation concerning the detriment of such deference. It appeared that more emphasis was placed on an individual and personality, more than God. People were being deceived and misguided, and the name of God was being misrepresented by leadership!

—All of sudden you start hearing about all of these so-called *spiritual fathers rising up*, and boasting about how many spiritual sons and daughters they have begat. And while I honestly believe that most of them meant well, a pervasive spirit of pride and deception crept in, and the vulnerable became as prey. This was a recipe for disaster! *The bible clearly says, "Neither give place to the devil." (Ephesians 4:29)*

We later begin to hear about a number of scandals in the church, and the abuse of power by leadership. It resonated within my spirit that something was not right about the position and perception of an individual claiming to be someone's spiritual Father!

This is not God's idea, but rather man's opportunity and importunity to exploit other people for their own personal gain. It is my belief that God never meant for man to be someone's spiritual father! *"He gave some to be Apostles, some Prophets, some Evangelists, some Pastors and Teachers", for the perfecting of the saints, for the work of the ministry, for the edifying of the Body of Christ; (Ephesians 4:11–12); But it never mentioned spiritual father!*

In Matthew Chapter 12:46–50, Jesus' mother and his brothers desired to speak to him. Jesus was addressed concerning his family desire to talk to him. But he replied, *who is my mother and brothers*? He then pointed to his disciples and said, here are my mother and my brothers. For whoever does the will of my *father in heaven* is my brother and sister and mother. I think it is noteworthy to observe that Jesus never said who is my father? He knew who his daddy was! *Jesus was not being disrespectful to his mother or brothers, but rather drawing the attention away from the earthly relationships to the more important spiritual relationships.*

I'm concerned about the direction of the Church culture, in particular, the relationship that is portrayed from leadership. For years, I have observed this "Identity Crisis", waiting for the Holy Spirit's timing to release it! I sure hope that this book will help somebody who may have lost their true identity in Christ to reclaim it.

"How hurtful it can be to deny one's true self and live a life of lies just to appease others."

—June Ahern

CHAPTER FOUR

Who Are You?

Two of the most significant questions a person can ask are, who am I, and whose am I? Do you really know who you are, especially who you are in Christ? If you don't know who you are, then there is a strong possibility that you don't know whose you are! If you don't know whose you are, then it's very easy for someone else to redefine your identity. So, the first thing I want to do before I go any further in this chapter is to affirm who you are and whose you are.

—You are a child of God! You are blessed and highly favored! You are God's treasured creation, and his wonderful masterpiece. You are fearfully and wonderfully made in the image of God, and you belong to the Lord. You are the head and not the tail, above and not beneath! You are the sons and daughters of the Most High God, Abba Father! You are an heir of God, and a joint-heir with Christ, which means you have a shared inheritance. Jesus is your elder brother and he is seated at the right hand of the Father making intercession for the saints, and that includes you! *When we fully understand the power of these statements, then we'll be truly free from the control and manipulation of manmade theology.*

Did you know that Fathers give identity to their children? In fact, most children legally carry their father's last name. I've even known of some fathers giving their last name to someone who's not their own biological child. Identity is significant both naturally and spiritually! People actually go through life seeking validation, and trying to figure out answers to the; who, what when, where, why, and how questions of life. This is quite normal behavior because everybody wants identity.

Some seek it from family, friends, co-workers, and many even seek it from the world. People look at T.V. personalities, social media, and even fictitious characters all in hopes of discovering their identity. People will dress a certain way or wear a certain hair style just to fit in and be accepted! Some have even gone to the extreme of plastic surgery in hopes of finding their identity. Someone once said, *"You are the sum total of the people you have in your closest inner circle",* and for some people that may not equate to a whole lot. Knowing who you are is very important, both genetically and spiritually.

One of the greatest challenges in today's religious climate is the fact that people don't know who they are, and more importantly whose they are! Sadly, many are perplexed about their identity, both spiritually and naturally. This confusion creates an opportunity for the vulnerable and unsuspecting to be manipulated! When a person is confused about their identity, they allow others to redefine them, or they will try to become someone else, and that's called identity theft!

It is human nature for us to want to trust other people, especially in religious circles. If this were not true, we would not hear about all of the horrible and tragic stories in our world. The truth is everybody is not out to get you, but there are some who seek to take you for everything you have! The word of God says in *Proverbs 3:5–6 "Trust in the Lord with all thine heart, and lean not to your own understanding. In all of your ways acknowledge him, and he shall direct your path."*

When God created you, He made you an original and not a copy. You are unique and distinct from all other human life! Your hand has its own fingerprints, your teeth has their own impressions, unlike any other person. God never intended for you to take another person's identity, neither did he intend for anyone to attempt to take his identity as our Father! Unfortunately, there is a lot of identity theft going on in the church, both literally and figuratively! Some people have trusted their leaders with their personal information and possessions, only to later become a victim. Many have been sexually and physically abused because they lost their identity to someone else!

Never lose your identity, except it be lost in Christ! Galatians 3: 26—"For in Christ Jesus you are all sons of God, through faith."

"If you allow people to tell you who you are, or who you aren't, you risk losing your true identity and living your entire life as a complete lie."

—John K. Vincent

CHAPTER FIVE

The Debilitating Disease
Called "Tradition"

Have you ever considered why people act the way that they act, and say some of the things they say, especially in religious affiliations? In many instances it's called learned behaviors, or just keeping with *tradition!* Remember the old saying, "Monkey see, monkey do?" The phrase makes reference to the learning of a process without the understanding of why it works. Sometimes it's just easier to follow our traditions even if we don't understand them, or if they're not biblically sound. I have come to the realization that there is an acute danger in some of the traditions of the church. Just to be clear, not all traditions are bad, but rest assured some are extremely dangerous.

Let me begin with a story that was shared with me many years go. There was a mother and daughter preparing Thanksgiving dinner for the family, and every year as a passed down tradition, the women would prepare the Turkey. One day the daughter asked her mother, why do you always cut the Turkey in half and only cook one half of the Turkey instead of the whole portion? The mother responded, because this is how my mother used to cook Turkeys when I was a little girl, so I've just continued the tradition!

The reason the daughter's grandmother cooked half the Turkey is because her small wood oven was not large enough to cook all of the Turkey at one time. This tradition was passed down from generation to generation without fully understanding the reason why it was done. Sometimes we do things without fully understanding why!—*Mark 7:13 says, "Making the word of God none effect through your tradition, which ye have delivered: and many such things do ye."*

A lack of understanding can create an abundance of confusion! Throughout history, interpretation of scriptures has always been a subject of great controversy. Whose interpretation or revelation of the scriptures is most accurate? For example, the scripture in Ephesians 6:1–2 says, *"Children, obey your parents in the Lord, for this is right. Honor thy Father and Mother which is the first commandment with promise"* but what does that scripture really mean?

Some may interpret this scripture as Paul inferring himself as a spiritual parent, and that would be the most logical interpretation. However, I would like to submit that the same scriptural text may suggest that children are to obey their natural parents who are in the Lord.

Paul gives an admonishment for children to obey godly parents, because if the parents are *"in the Lord"*, they will not ask their children to do what goes against the laws of God; and if they were, the children would not be obligated to obey them.

Children are protected from the consequence of their parent's willful violation of the laws of God. Is it possible that this topic was a discussion Paul had to address concerning the family dynamic? It is so important for us to read the bible with a very clear understanding so that we can rightly divide the word of truth and not the word of tradition. *Understanding of biblical text must transcend the contextual narrative.*

In today's church culture, scriptures must go beyond the literal context of the biblical narrative, and reach the depths of our own personal circumstances. *"That which is foundational in principle is also progressive in practices."* There are many lessons found in the word of God to help address our present issues, however we need the guidance of the Holy Spirit to give clarity and understanding of truth. All tradition is not good!

Oftentimes it is counterproductive to the development and advancement of our spiritual journey. Remember, our identity must never be lost in the 'traditions of men', except those traditions are sanctioned by God.

"There is a profound loyalty to ignorance; people will do anything they're asked without asking questions and seeking moral clarity."

—John K. Vincent

CHAPTER SIX
Who Is Your Daddy—*"Spiritual Father?"*

*(Disclaimer: What I'm about to say in this
chapter will challenge some people's theology)*

Who is your Spiritual Father? This question has become very complex for some. Perhaps you believe your pastor is your spiritual Father! Maybe the person that you really admire in ministry because they helped you become the man or woman of God you are today! The reality is that there are many people in the church who are totally oblivious to the truth! Please don't take that in a negative or condescending way!

Let's begin with John 4:24 which says, *"God is a spirit, or God is spirit—and they that worship him must worship him in spirit and in truth."* Do we really understand this text? To worship actually means to reverence or to give adoration to a deity. God is not a human being with a physical or human presence but rather a divine being. When Jesus was in the earth, he was God manifested in the flesh, yet he was not his own Father. God is spirit and deity, and He is our heavenly father!

The words that Jesus spoke in John 10:30 says, "I and my Father are one." Yet Jesus understood his earthly position that he was not his own daddy or superior to God. People who claim to be someone's spiritual father are carelessly placing themselves in the category of deity. Although this may not be intentional, it is extremely dangerous because it can lead to a spirit of idolatry, and open doors for the enemy!

I understand the context for which many may use the term, but I believe it is more detrimental than beneficial. A "Spiritual Father" does not have the same meaning in the way that some use it, therefore context is important. It's not just about semantics, but it's all about discernment and clarity! I do not believe for one minute that God is pleased with those who knowingly or unknowingly refer to themselves as a Spiritual Father!

Let's go a little deeper, as we take a look at Hebrews 12:9–10;— *"Furthermore we have had fathers of our flesh which corrected us, and we gave them reverence: shall we not much rather be in subjection unto the Father of Spirits, and live? For they verily for a few days chastened us after their own pleasure; but he for our profit, that we may be partakers of holiness."*

Notice how the scripture says, *we have had fathers (plural) of our <u>flesh</u> which corrected us and chastened us after their own pleasure.* This is an important statement to observe because it demonstrates how the *fathers of the flesh* disciplined according to their own desires. Fathers here are seen as the past generation of leaders.

Interestingly, the narrative shifts immediately from the fathers of flesh, to the Father *(singular)* of <u>Spirits</u>? I had never read this scripture in the manner that God revealed it to me. God is our Spiritual Father not our earthly father, and since we are spirit, soul and body, then God is the Father of our Spirits.

Earthly fathers give earthly advice and discipline that seems good at the time, but may not always be profitable in the end. Our Spiritual Father however gives heavenly advice that is always right! The chastening of our Spiritual Father is always to produce peaceful fruits of righteousness, a lifestyle of holiness, and an attitude that conforms to the will and purpose of God. The contrast of earthly fathers to our "Spiritual Father" is quite apparent, and demonstrates the proper context of relationship.

Hebrews 12:7 says,—*"If ye endure chastening, God dealeth with you as with sons; for what son is he whom the father chasteneth not? But if ye be without chastisement, whereof all are partakers, then are ye bastards, and not sons."*—Are you a bastard, or are you a legitimate child of God?

In John Chapter 8 Jesus demonstrates that real discipleship depends on having the right Father! After having identified the true disciples that believed in him, Jesus later addressed the Jews who didn't believe, and explained to them that they had the wrong Father. They had claimed Abraham as their Father, but Jesus made clear to them that they were just Abraham's physical seed.

Jesus later stated in John 8:44, *"Ye are of your father the devil, and the lusts of your father ye will do, He was a murderer from the beginning, and abode not in the truth because there is no truth in him. When he speaketh a lie, he speaketh of his own: for he is a liar and the father of it."*

To call any earthly man a spiritual father is not only an insult to God, but very resemblance of when Satan tried to equal and even exalt himself above God. If someone else is your so-called spiritual father, then who is God?

In fact, when acknowledging someone as your spiritual father, one is more likely to depend on that individual than to depend on Jehovah. God is our heavenly Father, but he is also our Spiritual Father! *God is not flesh, God is a "Spirit! We all have one earthly father, and I believe we all have one Spiritual father.*

The Greek word for Father is *"Pateras" or Pater in Latin*, which actually means one who imparts life, and is the source of life. God is the only one who is the total source of life. When someone is designated as your total source, they are placed in a position which essentially replaces God! No human being is worthy of such a title because they are not capable of providing for the total needs of man; spirit, soul, and body. In fact, the only one who is able to do such is, *Abba Father*, and *I call him Daddy!*

First, let's revisit when we were born again: we were born of the spirit and not of the flesh. We repented of our sins and confessed Jesus, God's only begotten son, as our Lord and Savior. We invited him to live in our hearts. We were adopted into the family of God, and by divine birthright, we became joint-heirs with Jesus Christ.

Second, we were blessed with all spiritual blessings according to *Ephesians 1:3–6,—"Blessed be the God and Father of our Lord Jesus Christ, who hath blessed us with all spiritual blessings in heavenly places in Christ: According as he hath chosen us in him before the foundation of the world that we should be holy and without blame before him in love: Having predestinated us unto the adoption of children by Jesus Christ to himself, according to the good pleasure of his will, to the praise of the glory of his grace, wherein he hath made us accepted in the beloved."*

Third, we are a triune being comprised of a spirit, soul, and body. Think about it from this perspective, if God is our Father, and Jesus is our elder brother, then how is it possible for anyone else to be considered our *"spiritual father?"* Do we think that our spiritual position is greater than that of Christ?

I have one earthly Father, who is now deceased. His name was John Vincent Jr., and he was a great Father, a beloved Bishop of the Lord's church, and one who did all that he could to ensure his family's spiritual heritage in Christ. He taught us how to love God with all of our hearts, and he preached the uncompromised gospel. He was my spiritual covering, advisor, and leader, but God and only God is my spiritual Father!

We must understand, God is our eternal Father who will never die! My earthly Father is no longer here to give me counsel, but my Spiritual Father continues to lead and guide me through the Holy Spirit. I'm concerned about leaders who want to be recognized as somebody's spiritual Father, when they have not demonstrated the ability to be good earthly Fathers! Why would God entrust you with the great responsibility of being anyone's spiritual father when you are not spiritual?

—*"For to be carnally minded is death but to be spiritually minded is life and peace. Because the carnal mind is enmity against God: for it is not subject to the law of God, neither indeed can be!" (Romans 8:6–7)*

The Apostle Paul says in First Timothy 3:5, *"For if a man know not how to rule his own house, how shall he take care of the church of God?"* There are far too many people in leadership who do not rule their own homes well! It is biblically wrong in my understanding of the sacred scriptures for a person to call themselves someone's spiritual father, but they have not ruled their own home well. God is a God of order and a God of Supreme Identity! His position exceeds all other earthly positions.

When Paul writes, in I Corinthians 4:15, "For though ye have ten thousand instructors in Christ, yet have ye not many fathers: for in Christ Jesus I have begotten you through the gospel."—What exactly is he saying? I believe Paul is saying here that he is a Father in the gospel, meaning he is the one responsible for having introduced those who were converts in Corinth to salvation, and responsible for their spiritual development. I further believe that Paul recognizes that he is not their total source! May I further submit to you that there is an acute difference between a "Father in the Gospel" and a "Spiritual Father?"

In Genesis Chapter 12, *Abram*, whose name was later changed to Abraham, was called the "Father of Faith" of the Hebrew Nation. God told him to move out of his country, away from his kindred and *father's* house. God promised to bless him, and to make his name great, and that he would be a blessing, not a *Spiritual Father. Romans 4:22 says, "And therefore it was imputed to him for righteousness."*

Reverend Dr. Martin Luther King Jr was a Baptist minister, who became known as the "Father of the Civil Rights Movement" in the 50's and 60's. He led the march to social justice and equality, and is forever recognized in history as a Transformational Leader. His influence reached all of the world, yet he was not a *"Spiritual Father."*

The Wright brothers are considered the "Fathers of Aviation" because they were the first to originate the airplane successfully. They discovered a faster way for people to travel from one place to another, and their legacy is forever cemented in aviation history, but they are not *"Spiritual Fathers."*

Saul, before he was converted had persecuted the early church and followers of Jesus, and even approved their killings, but later became the Apostle Paul, and a "Father in the Gospel" to his sons Timothy and others, but he too was not a *"Spiritual Father."*

Many denominations refer to the aged or mature women in the church as Mothers, and the men as Fathers of the church, but there is a distinction in identifying one as a spiritual father. I have had personal conversations with friends of mine who claim to have spiritual sons and daughters. I love them and respect their ministries, but I respectfully disagree with that position.

Some have even gone as far as saying that they have spiritual grandsons and granddaughters or spiritual nieces and nephews. As I listened, I would find myself pondering on how one could have so many spiritual children. In Christ Jesus we are all brothers and sisters in the family of God. Jesus said in *Matthew 23:9 and 11 "And call no man your father upon the earth: for one is your Father, which is in heaven... But he that is greatest among you shall be your servant!*—So then, the appropriate title for leaders is really, *Servant-Leader*!

The word "Father" denotes so much more than what many perceive. If one is not capable of providing for *every* need, then they are not qualified to be called a "Spiritual Father!" Perhaps you are a Spiritual leader, a mentor, a covering but not a Spiritual Father. You may be a father in the gospel, or a father of a movement. No spiritual leader, including the Pope, the Bishops of a denomination, Senior Pastors, or any other leadership position should ever make the mistake of referring to themselves, or encouraging others to refer to them as a Spiritual Father!

Jesus gives a very clear explanation as to why no one should call any man on earth who spiritually guides them their father! Matthew 23:7–8—"they love to receive respectful greetings as they walk in the marketplaces, and to be called of men 'Rabbi, Rabbi. But be not ye called Rabbi, for one is your Master, even Christ, <u>and all ye all brethren</u>.

It's interesting that Christ identified himself as our elder brother, even though he and the father were one. How can a person be someone's spiritual father and brother at the same time? Let me dig a little deeper. How can one call himself a "spiritual father" and sleep with his spiritual sons and daughters. That would be considered spiritual incest, right? Let's take it a step further. How many "Spiritual Fathers" can you have? People are so quick to get offended and leave from under one leadership and then go to someone else declaring them as their spiritual father. My brothers and sisters it doesn't work that way!

Some of you may remember "Jim Jones." He was an American religious cult leader. His story is quite riveting! I personally believe that he initially meant well in the onset of his ministry, but he later became intoxicated with his own flesh and started identifying himself as the people's messiah. He deceived so many people of African American descent because of their ignorance and vulnerability. He seduced the people, and sadly, more than 900 hundred lives were lost to mass suicide.

I could go on and on about the term "Spiritual Father", and the detriment it has caused to the church. I'm sure some will continue with their tradition, but I want to caution, those who continue, do so at their own risk!" I believe that God is our "Spiritual Father", and we who are in leadership have an obligation to always point our parish to Him!

Hosea 4:6—"My people are destroyed for lack of knowledge: because thou hast rejected knowledge, I will also reject thee, that thou shalt be no priest to me: seeing thou hast forgotten the law of thy God, I will also forget thy children."

When the church lacks discernment, anyone can be susceptible to a wrong spirit!

—John K. Vincent

CHAPTER SEVEN

DNA Reveals: *"You are not the Father"*

Y ou may be familiar with the daytime television show *Maury*, or some of the other "Paternity Court" shows, in which the Judge reveals the DNA test for paternity. The anticipation of the results oftentimes leads to a flood of emotions for all parties involved. When the paternity results are positive, the father is legally and morally responsible for the emotional, physical, and financial well-being of the child. However, when the results are negative, the presumed father is released from all responsibilities. To all of you who are spiritual coverings in the Body of Christ, the paternity test results are in, and you are not the Father! Thank God that you're not, because it alleviates some of the unnecessary stress and anxiety that some of you have been carrying for a long time.

God never meant for you to identify yourself as someone's spiritual father. While it is a very common practice in the Catholic Church to reference the priest as *"Holy Father"*, it is not scriptural, and has contributed to the Identity Crisis we see in our world today. Unfortunately, people tend to place their total confidence and trust in another human being, and consequently they get caught up in a compromised or abusive relationship.

We all have been made aware of the various scandals surrounding many of the Catholic priest, and the countless lawsuits that have been filed for those who were victims of sexual abuse. The same has been in the Protestant reformations, and many have been fatally wounded throughout the Body of Christ. I want to be very clear that my assertions are not on the merit of head knowledge, but rather a divine mandate to address and help heal the Body of Christ at large. Only God is omniscient, and knows all. Only God is omnipresent, everywhere all the time. Only God is Omnipotent, having all power! Only God is our Spiritual Father!

Who is your "spiritual daddy?" Who is the person that has control of your heart and mind? I know this kind of thinking might go against traditional beliefs of what has been taught, yet I believe that when we say it right, we can get it right!

We must be guarded that we don't become possessive of God's people. If they are born of the spirit and of the water, and confessed Jesus as their Lord, then they have God's DNA, and they are his sons and daughters, not ours! *Therefore, we are not the Father!*

Since we know we are not the Father, no leader should ever assume a spiritual role in someone's life in which they become possessive of the individuals they lead. Neither should one seek a position greater than what they are equipped and anointed by God to handle. Whenever a person becomes possessive of the people they lead, it crosses spiritual boundaries, and fosters an unhealthy relationship that creates a recipe for disaster!

A "Cataclysm" by definition is a catastrophic and violent event in the world that causes abrupt change, and alters what is considered to be a normal environment, oftentimes left in permanent ruins. Many are aware of the natural disasters in the world, such as earthquakes, tornados, tsunamis, and hurricanes, however there are also some "spiritual disasters", and these disasters disrupt the foundation of or fundamental beliefs and practices, adversely changing the identity of church culture. The church culture should reflect that of Christ, and the Kingdom of God.

"Propaganda" is the use of information, ideas, facts, and many times lies to promote one's point of view, while reshaping the mentality and behaviors of those under their influence. It is a cunning way of conditioning the minds of people to relinquish their identity and individuality. This is how people are deceived and manipulated, both in government and in the church.

Our goal as Christian leaders should never be to usurp authority, neither should we seek to influence public opinion with information that is misleading or biased. Rather, we should always seek the advancement of the God's Kingdom without any hidden agendas. Never forget that those who are in authority are also those that are under the authority of God. For there is no other authority higher or equal to the position and power of God. Praise God that we don't have to carry that burden.

"He that is short and to the point is wise"

—John K. Vincent

CHAPTER EIGHT
"Say it Right, Portray it Right"

C an you think of a time in your life that you said something without considering how others would be affected? Perhaps you meant to say what you said, but it's how you said it that was incorrect. Words are containers that carry power to build or to tear down! We must choose our words very carefully. What you say is just as important as how you say, and what you think is just as important as how you act! Our actions do speak louder than our words, but our words can create barriers. Jesus said in Matthew 12:37 *"For by your words you shall be justified, and by your words you shall be condemned."*

There are many scriptures to support our respective ideologies and opinions, and some of us can quote them very well! However, as God-ordained leaders, it is not our responsibility to be someone's Spiritual

Father because that is God's designated role! It is our responsibility to be a good example, leader, teacher, counselor, and advisor, and it's important that we portray in private what we profess in public!

The apostle Paul encouraged Timothy, his mentee in the faith in I Timothy 4:12; *"Let no man despise thy youth, but be thou an example for the believers in speech, in conduct, in love, in faith and in purity."* There are times in all of our lives when we need affirmation and validation. Everybody likes to have encouragement from others, and a little encouragement can go a long ways!

Let's examine what it mean to be a son or daughter in the Faith? For some leaders it appears to mean total control over the people while seeking opportunity for material gain. However, those who understand the role and assignment of a shepherd understand that they are the watchman of one's soul! A Godly shepherd who is sincerely concerned about the sheep would never intentionally harm the flock in which they are called to lead.

—Jeremiah 3:15 says, *"And I will give you pastors (not fathers) according to mine heart, which shall feed you with knowledge and understanding."* Sheep need shepherds or pastors, not spiritual fathers. It's true that we are spiritual beings, and there are many pastors that have a fathering heart, but don't ever forget that only God is our Spiritual Father!

Sometimes we adopt certain sayings and beliefs because of what we have traditionally observed of others, but may I conclude this brief chapter by saying, GOD is our Spiritual daddy and Heavenly Father, Jesus is our elder brother, and he has entrusted those of us who shepherd the flock to be good watchmen and servant leaders! Let's make sure we 'Say it Right', because our words and actions matter!

A half-truth is a whole lie!

—Unknown

CHAPTER NINE
"Reclaiming Spiritual Identity"

This last chapter may not apply to everyone, but for many of you it will! So much has already been shared in the previous chapters concerning the identity crisis in the church and the religious propaganda that has adversely impacted her image. Countless of lives have been forever scarred by people who are intoxicated with their own desire for power and control of others. Many people have fallen victim to these imposters in the church, who use their gifts, glorified titles and sphere of influence as a means of manipulating and taking advantage of innocent people. These things should never be named among the saints!

The reality is that many people today are still suffering from post-traumatic symptoms caused from years of mental, physical, emotional, financial, sexual and spiritual abuse. There are some stories that will never be told because they were carried to the grave, and there are others that are simply too painful to rehearse. Some people have left the church as a result of their injury, but they still have faith in Jesus. Others have totally abandoned their belief in God, and want nothing to do with religion. Regardless, God's grace is yet sufficient! His power is still able to heal and restore from the shame and the pain of the past!

Maybe you were very naive and vulnerable at one time, but I declare right now you are much stronger, wiser, and better! Your past experiences does not and will not define your present opportunities, neither does it negate your future possibilities. There is still a plan and a purpose for your life and all you must do is embrace the will of God for you!

One of the fastest way to reclaim your spiritual identity is to first acknowledge that you lost it! You allowed someone else to give you an identity and you lost focus. I know you didn't mean to, and you don't even have to justify, rationalize, or even minimize the fact that you forgot who you were in Christ! Just own it, repent of it, and move on! Acceptance is not always easy but it's absolutely imperative in order to move forward. Release the people who offended you and embrace peace.—Psalm 119:165 says, *"Great peace have they that love thy law, and nothing shall offend them."*

—Mark 11:25 *"And when you stand praying, if you have anything against anyone, forgive him that your Father in heaven may also forgive you your trespasses."*

Forgiveness is not a request but it's a commandment of God. If you want to be forgiven then you must forgive others. Forgiveness does not mean you invite the person who wronged you to do it again. Forgiveness does not mean that you cover up and pretend that nothing ever happened. Forgiveness is understanding the heart of God! It is an act of mercy and compassion, in the same way God demonstrated his love toward all of us.

When we forgive others, we free ourselves from the pain and agony of our past, from the power and control of others, and from the masks and facades we try to hide behind. It may not always seem easy to let go, but when you release all the tension and friction, it will give you extended life and freedom; and then the real healing process will begin!

Let me conclude by declaring this over your life, you will never be confused about your spiritual identity again. You know who you are, and most importantly whose you are. You are a Child of God destined for victory! You are a joint-heir with Jesus Christ! You have been given power and authority as a believer to fulfill your assignment in the earth.

You will never allow any man or woman to claim spiritual ownership over your soul, nor control of your mind, body or spirit. Your Spiritual Father is God, who resides in heaven, and is capable of supplying all of your natural needs in the earth. Your worship shall be unto God and him only! Your teacher is the Holy Spirit who resides within in you, and empowers you for success and effective witnessing in the earth. You will honor and respect your spiritual leaders, and pray for them as God's honorable servants, but you will never fall into the entrapment of idolizing and worshipping any man again!—*No More Identity Crisis!*

—*John 8:36 "So if the son sets you free, you will be free indeed."*

ABOUT THE AUTHOR

Bishop John K. Vincent, Doctorate of Ministry/Leadership, is a highly respected pastor and community leader who resides in Nashville, TN. He is the senior pastor and founder of Greater Compassion Ministries Church Inc., the presiding overseer of UFAM (United Fellowship Alliance of Ministries), as well as the president of Greater Compassion Community Initiatives, a (501c3) nonprofit organization. He has been in ministry nearly 40 years, and was consecrated to the episcopacy on October 26, 2018. He lends his voice and gifts to the church as a voice of spiritual clarity and conformance to the image of Christ.

Bishop Vincent is a second-generation preacher, a graduate of the prestigious Oral Roberts University, where he earned a bachelor of science in mass media communications, as well as concentrated studies in biblical history and Christian literature. He holds a master of business administration from the University of Phoenix, and is currently working on a doctorate of ministry at Birmingham Theological Seminary.

In addition to being an author, a prolific song-writer and composer, gospel preacher and teacher, he is an entrepreneur who enjoys using his talents to serve in the community, and continues to make a legible imprint in the lives of people.

His greatest pride and joy are his lovely wife of 31 years, their three children, and one grandchild. His value of faith, love for God and people is evident in his life.